Contents

CHAPTER 1

  Introduction

    The 1987 Crash

  ETFs from Evolution to Revolution

    The Creation and Development of Exchange-Traded Funds in North America

    The Market for ETFs in Europe

CHAPTER 2

  Understanding how ETFs operate

    Define ETFs

    How ETFs work

    ETFs' Potential benefits

CHAPTER 3

  Best ETF trading (making money) strategies

    Dollar-Cost Averaging

    Asset Allocation

    Use ETFs to Gain Exposure to an Industry

    Foreign ETF Assets Enable You to Access the International Markets

    Invest in Commodities

    Bond ETFs are a Gift that Just Keeps on Giving

    Exchange-Traded Notes

    Trade the Currency Market with ETFs

    Hedging Risk with ETFs

    Hedging

    Consider ETF Options

    Trade Earnings Season with ETFs

    Trade ETFs Which Fit Your Investment Style

    Swing Trading

- Sector Rotation
- Selling Short

CHAPTER 4

- ETF structure and asset class issues
  - DEFINING THE MARKET
  - Exchange-Traded Product (ETP)
  - Unit Investment Trust
  - Commodities Pool
  - Exchange-Traded Note
  - Counterparty Risk
  - Exchange-Traded Notes
  - Swaps
  - Derivatives
  - Securities Lending
  - TAX RISK
  - ETF TAX PRIMER
  - Fixed-Income and Equity ETFs
  - Commodity ETFs
  - Currency ETFs
- Types of Exchange-Traded Portfolios
  - Equity Funds
  - Fixed-Income Funds
  - Commodity Funds
  - Currency Funds
  - Real Estate Funds
  - Specialty Funds
  - Quick Note on ETFs vs. Mutual Funds

CHAPTER 5

- Conclusion and Perspectives

CHAPTER 1

Introduction

The creation of Exchange-Traded Funds (ETFs) is among the most distinctive successes in financial innovation since the emergence of financial futures. Like index funds, the main goal is to replicate as closely as possible the efficiency of their benchmark indices. As contrary to the traditional mutual funds, Exchange-Traded Funds are also listed on the exchange and are traded intra-daily. Exchanges and issuers meant for the diversifying opportunities that are provided to every kind of investor at flexible and affordable cost, whilst highlighting their transparency, low management fees, and tax efficiency. Most of these attributes depend on a particular "in-kind" creation and redemption principle: You can continuously create new shares when you deposit a portfolio of stocks that closely approximate holdings of the fund and investors can redeem the outstanding ETF shares while in return receiving the basket portfolio. The holdings are transparent because the fund portfolios are revealed at the end of each day of trading.

ETFs were first introduced on Canadian and U.S. exchanges in the early 1990s. For the first few years, only a small fraction of the managed assets in index funds was represented. However, there was an average annual growth rate of 132% of ETF assets from the year 1995 - 2001 (Gastineau, 2002) shows the rising importance of these instruments. In 1999 Cubes was launched and came along with dramatic growth in the volume traded, which made the major ETFs some of the most traded equity securities actively on the United States stock exchanges. The ETF markets Since then, have continuously grown, not just in the variety and number of products, but in terms of market and asset value as well. Before then, they were looking to replicate new ETFs extended their specialty to sectors, broad-based stock indices, fixed-income instruments, international markets, and most recently commodities.

In late 2005, they listed 453 Exchange-Traded Funds all over the world for assets worth $343B. In the United States, total ETF assets added up to $296.02B, as compared to $8.9T in the mutual funds. Initially, ETFs were developed in the United States by the American Stock Exchange and soon faced trading competition. Before the New York Stock Exchange ventured into ETFs, the securities were already trading on the regional exchanges, the Island Electronic

Crossing Network and the Nasdaq Intermarket. Even though they were long opposed to the ETFs, for the first time in the history of the NYSE it began to trade the three most active ETFs under the Unlisted Trading Privileges in 2001 July 31st.

Besides, various trading venues competed for the listings as well. The Nasdaq-100 Index Tracking Stocks also referred to as "Cubes" on December 1st, 2004, changed the listing to Nasdaq from the AMEX. Lately, in 2005, July 20th, Barclays Global Investors revealed that they wanted to transfer 61 iShares Exchange-Traded Funds to the New York Stock Exchange from the America stock Exchange. Despite receiving extraordinary press coverage, just a handful of academic studies were committed to the research of ETFs before 2000. The spectacular growth ETFs experienced can be attributed to the launch of Cubes where more extensive research focused more on these securities.

There is existing competition between ETFs and index securities: index futures, options contracts, and index component stocks, and naturally, closed-end funds and index mutual funds. ETFs may be majorly viewed as highly redundant assets that shouldn't influence the prevailing existing equilibriums. Nevertheless, their success alludes to filling a gap in the investors' requirements. The considerable volume of trading is likely to affect the markets of the relevant securities. Study in the ETFs is built based on three main subjects, all the studies are based on an empirical viewpoint:

- Does the ETFs represent a performing alternative to traditional index mutual funds?
- Does the ETF particular structure allow more flexible and efficient index fund pricing?
- what is the impact of the advent of the ETFs on the market and trading quality relative to index derivatives and index component stocks?

Other empirical research focuses on ETFs and investigates the diverse subjects as well, like the competition between the shape of the demand curve, the use of ETFs or trading venues.

The 1987 Crash

October 19 of 1987 was the Black Monday, the Dow Jones Industrial Average dropped more than 20% in just a day. It was going to be the 2nd-largest single-day percent decline in the history of the stock market. The biggest single-day decline happened on December 12th of 1914, when the Dow Jones Industrial Average dropped 24%. But, the 1914 event could be explained. The NYSE had not opened for 6 months since the beginning of World War I, and many individuals were eagerly waiting to sell when the opening bell goes. Now, different from 1914 one, the 1987 crush looked like it started from nothing of importance (no trigger). There were no major events or news before the fall and the political environment in DC was quite benign. The then-President Reagan was in his 7th year in office, and other than the Afghanistan Soviet occupation, there were no major conflicts that were threatening the peace of the world. The common most used excuse of the 1987 crash was program traders selling. Program traders used computer tracking of market movements which is an automated buy or sell system. The system involved instant implementation of orders in huge blocks of futures and stocks. Other economists said that the collapse was due to program trading, while others refuted and said that the programs had very little impact on it. The strategy, either way, was the scapegoat and took most of the blame for the crush. As a result of Black Monday, one thing became clear, that the big institutional investors didn't have enough liquidity that they required to hedge positions quickly. Therefore, markets across the globe were restricted in their trading. When the stock fell, the options and futures and markets were temporarily closed, and if the stock fell more, then the SE was closed.

The futures and options markets were also included due to the liquidity can dry quickly up in those markets in case of a crisis, and this can cause equities to go lower. Closing of markets was the first circuit breaker to salvage the cascade of the stock selling. In case that doesn't work, the regulators then decided that the SEs should just stop trading. The circuit breakers were reactive in a crisis to the issue of limited liquidity, but there was no really easy or quick way to come up with solutions. What was required was reliable and a simple way to hedge the portfolio of stocks, by the use of the exchange-traded vehicle. The closed-end funds trade on a SE, but there was an issue. Using them for hedging against the quickly declining stock values. The market value of a closed-end fund is known by the supply and demand for that particular fund, not the underlying Net Asset Value of the fund stocks. As a result, the market value of a closed-end fund could become extremely discounted to the relative NAV when markets decline. Depending on the suddenness of the fall and the fund, the NAV discount could go as high as 30%, and it could maintain this position for a very long time. Sellers who use closed-end funds to hedge against the stock positions are most likely selling at built-in losses. Closed-end funds can have a premium or discount frequently because the fund cannot redeem shares from the selling investors when funds are at a discount or provide extra shares to the new investors when funds are at a premium. Closed-end fund companies can't self-deal in their funds as well. Since the number of shares is fixed, there is no way to arbitrage the difference between the NAV and the fund price. If such a mechanism existed, it would cause the market value of the closed-end fund to align with the underlying Net Asset Value, as investors arbitrage fund shares for the stock shares and the other way around. Closed-end fund premiums and discounts would go away if arbitrage were allowed to happen. For instance, if a fund were able to redeem closed-end shares while they are selling at a discount to Net Asset Value, the manager could then simultaneously sell off the underlying securities which make up the fund at real-time values and make a risk-free profit for remaining investors in the fund. And if the market value of the fund sold at a premium to Net Asset Value, then more closed-end fund shares could be sold by the manager on the open market and simultaneously buy the underlying securities that make up the fund at market value that is lower, resulting to risk-free a profit arbitrage.

ETFs from Evolution to Revolution

Exchange-traded funds rose from their fledgling start in 1993 to a whole revolution in the mutual fund sector. The number of Exchange-Traded Funds offerings is growing every year. From 2004, the number of ETFs that were available for investment doubled in their numbers about every 18 months. No one really knows when this growth will start to slow down. However, there are all reasons to believe, that all of ETFs are going to double or triple again before they can start any slowdown. As more individuals get enlightened on the benefits of ETFs and put their investment in them, other potential investors want to understand how these distinctive products can be suited to their portfolios. The most ideal place to start the study of the ETFs is right from the beginning. This book highlights the events which can lead to the creation of the ETFs, and how the industry has evolved over the past few years. The book takes us to a place in evolution that we are today, and looks at the places the sector is likely headed to in the future.

The Creation and Development of Exchange-Traded Funds in North America

Judging from how restrictive authors are in the definitions, ETFs, as we know them now, were introduced first in the early 90s, in either Canada (with TIPs that were traded first in 1990) or maybe three years later in the United State (with SPDRs). However, being able to trade an entire stock basket in just one transaction goes further back. Major United States brokerage firms offered program trading facilities back in the late '70s, specifically for the S&P 500 index. Program trading became more common, With the introduction of index futures contracts. This allowed coming up with a more ideal instrument to allow index elements to be negotiated in just one trade became more interesting.

In 1989, the Philadelphia Stock Exchange and the AMEX began to trade Index Participation Shares (IPS). Those synthetic instruments were meant to replicate the performance and functions of the S&P 500 index, and other indexes, but they had the same features as those of the futures contracts. Despite the keen interest from investors, Index Participation Shares had to put to an end trading after a lawsuit filed by the Commodity Futures Trading Commission (CFTC) and the Chicago Mercantile Exchange was won. IPS as a futures contract was only to be traded on the futures exchange that was regulated by the Commodity Futures Trading Contract.

The Toronto Index Participation Units (TIPs), the 1st equity kind of index fund, was on March 9th, 1990 introduced on the Toronto Stock Exchange. Tracking of the Toronto was traded on the Toronto stock exchange and was featured with extremely affordable management fees, seeing that the manager of the fund was authorized to issue a loan to stocks held by the fund, which demand was normally high. This item was followed by HIPs in 1994, founded on the entire FTSE-100 index. Aside from the high success of the securities, their extremely low expense ratios at the end of the day made them very expensive for the exchange and its clients. HIPs and TIPs were ended in 2003. In 1993, after 3 years of conflict with the SEC, the American Stock Exchange (AMEX) began trading S&P's 500 Depositary Receipt (SPDR, commonly referred to as the "Spider", ticker SPY), it is in mostly known as the world's 1st ETF. The fund was sponsored by an AMEX subsidiary PDR Services Corporation, that State Street Bank and Trust as a trustee. Its particular trust trading process and structure that was made up of a model for the upcoming ETFs introduced, like Diamonds (ticker DIA), MidCap SPDRs, Select Sector SPDRs, or based on the Dow Jones Industrial Average. In 1996, a mutual fund arrangement for the WEBS (World Equity Benchmark Shares), ETFs that showed the performance of the foreign market's indices, were preferred by Barclays Global Investors. Aside from the growing interest, it had to take a few years for the funds to take off.

The ETF sector experienced an effective boom in 1999 March when the Nasdaq-100 Index Tracking Stock was launched, commonly known as Qubes or Cubes relative to its previous ticker, QQQ, which recently metamorphosed to QQQQ. In the second year of its trading, Cube was trading an average daily of 70 million shares, which is about 4% of what Nasdaq trade. The increasing popularity of this particular fund enhanced the awareness of the other ETFs and all the assets under management increased by more than doubled in the year 2000, up to $70B at the end of the same year (Gallagher and Frino, 2001). From that time, the growth in ETFs has not shown any signs to slow down in the United States: 2001 it was 27%,

2002 it was 23%, 2003 it was 48%, 2004 it was 50%, and even remained high in 2005 at 31%. As the years progressed, ETF assets progressively became the alternative to the conventional non-traded index mutual funds that led their key competitors like Fidelity or Vanguard to bring down their fees to a 10 basis point or even less.

Before the close of 2002, 113 ETFs were in the United States with roughly $102.14B in assets that were under management. And before the close of 2006, with new ETF assets based on the more diverse kind of indices launched and new cash invested in the already existing ETFs, the ETF sector consisted of 4 SE with $335 billion in assets from a listing of 216 ETFs. The sponsored by Barclays Global Investors (iShares) and sponsored by State Street Global Advisors (StreetTracks) series show a very diversified offer of all the countries and/or sectors, but the ETFs are dominated by Cube, Diamond, and Spider, that is founded on the relatively wide market indexes. The trading volume focuses on the 2 most popular ETFs, Spiders, and Cubes, with annual turnovers of as high as 400% for the former and 700% for the latter, this is according to (Bogle, 2004). Which makes Cubes, the most ideal passive instrument to invest, and the most actively traded that was listed on the equity security in the United States in 2005, with an average of $97 M shares traded daily.

The Market for ETFs in Europe

The European stock exchanges begun listing their first Exchange-Traded Funds in the year 2000, long after they had gained popularity in the United States. The London Stock Exchange and Deutsche Börse were among the 1st exchanges to quote ETF assets in Europe in 2000 April. With the opening of the extraMARK and XTF particular market segments. Competition intensified rapidly when the Stockholm Stock Exchange entered the market at the end of 2000 October, Euronext on 2001 January, this is when NextTrack started trading ETF assets first in Amsterdam and Paris marketplaces, (In Brussels trading started in 2002 October) and of the Swiss Stock Exchange on 2001 March. In 2002 February, Helsinki Stock Exchange then listed its first ETF asset (IHEX 35), and in September of the same year, the Borsa Italiana began the MTF segment that was dedicated to ETFs. Much later in 2004 December, ETFs were then launched in the Icelandic market, in 2005 March they were opened in the Norwegian market, while the Irish market opened on 2005 April and in 2005 November the Austrian market was launched.

By the end of the year 2005, 11 exchanges had listed at least 160 ETF assets, with the growth of the assets at an annual growth of up to €45 billion at a rate of 60%. Following a similar trend as those observed in the United States, exchanges started by quoting wide-based regional and national equity index ETF assets. They at once diversified their benchmarks to different underlying indices. For instance, after only 6 and 5 years, respectively, the Deutsche Börse and Euronext listed 95 and 77 ETF assets.

This also included ETF assets based on European or eurozone indices, advent country indices, style (growth, mid-caps, socially responsible, small caps, value, etc.) or industry indices.

Aside from the equity-based ETF assets, the sponsors launched ETFs based on precious metals, commodities and lastly fixed-income ETFs.

Exchange	ETFs			Monthly average trading volume	
	Number of ETFs	Number of underlying indices	Number of issuers	Number of trades	Amount traded (K€)
Deutsche Börse	77	68	9	18,787	3,842.1
Euronext	95	68	10	14,434	1,481.9
London Stock Exchange	28	28	1	#N/A	770.2
Borsa Italiana	30	29	5	29,964	727.1
SWX Swiss Exchange	34	26	8	6,383	524.3
Virt-X	17	17	4	552	59.8
OMX	11	11	2	744	28.7
Wiener Börse	11	10	2	119	19.6
Oslo Børs	2	2	1	45	1.9

Overview of the European ETF Markets, 2005

The above table shows ETF trading on the European marketplaces for the year 2005. The Euronext and Deutsche Börse account for at least 70% of all the amount traded in ETF assets in Europe. On the Deutsche Börse, an average monthly of €3,842 million was traded in 2005 VS an average of €1,481 million on the Euronext, even though fewer ETF assets were listed on the popular exchange at that time. Despite its growing continuously, the figures are still not near those that were observed in the United States. Interestingly, the Borsa Italiana is the leader in the number of trades, with roughly twice as many transactions per month as the Euronext and Deutsche Börse, but it was only worth €0,524 M. This then shows the difference in the kind of European ETF markets investors. In the 1st 2 markets, the volume traded basically comes from the institutional investors who post bigger orders, but for the Italian market, it is characterized by a large proportion of retail trader (individual investors) who post significantly small orders. The above table also shows the competition existing between exchanges regarding the order flows in of ETF assets and between the issuers of the attraction of the new investments made. The LSE is the only one that has a single ETF series in the European marketplace, the iShares sponsored by Barclays Global Investors. In all other exchanges, many different issuers manage ETF assets based on either under license from index providers or particular "home" indices. The former represents the majority of the ETF assets that are listed in Europe, with indices from FTSE, STOXX, iBoxx or MSCI who grant multiple licenses sometimes to the competing issuers. For instance, the 95 ETF assets issued by 10 sponsors which are traded on the Euronext track only the performance of 68 various underlying indices. As in the United States, the major regional (Dow Jones STOXX 50, Dow Jones EURO STOXX 50) and national (the English FTSE 100, the French CAC 40) indices focus most on the assets under management and also the volume traded. Typically, other ETF assets utilize these indices as benchmark and are sometimes listed on the same exchange or different European exchanges. The table below shows the basic information on the ETF assets tracking the DJ Euro STOXX 50 and the CAC 40 indices competing on the NextTrack as of Dec 31st of 2005. It looks like even if those ETF assets are traded mostly on the Euronext, the average number of daily transactions is low and highly focused on the single ETF asset for every index. If similar observation works for the assets under management of the CAC 40 index with at least €3 B, that doesn't apply to the DJ Euro STOXX 50. As for this eurozone index, 3 ETF assets, issued by Barclays, IndExchange, and Lyxor, have assets that are greater than €3 B under their management. Nevertheless, the volume traded still mostly focuses on the single ETF asset. This kind of situation is common of the cross the listing of ETF assets in Europe (DJ Euro STOXX 50-based ETF assets that are listed on seven different exchanges) where the issuers profit from both their own nation on their country market and more imperatively, from their anteriority. Investors seem to keep on trading on the same ETF asset even if competitors launch on the same indices as them.

ETF	Issuer	Management fess	Dividend frequency	Trading volume			Assets under management	
				# trades.	# shares	Amount (K€)	# shares (thousands)	Amount (K€)
Underlying index: CAC 40								
Lyxor ETF CAC 40	Lyxor AM	0.25%	annual	242	466,805	19,856.83	67,831.75	3,233,539
CAC40 indexis (02/03/05)	Crédit Agricole AM	0.25%	annual	9	45,375	1,883.48	14,227.28	680,170
EasyETF CAC40 (17/03/05)	AXA IM, BNP Paribas	0.25%	annual	12	107,997	4,719.19	17,800.00	840,516
Underlying index: DJ Euro STOXX 50								
Lyxor ETF DJ Euro STOXX 50	Lyxor AM	0.25%	annual	85	544,386	17,425.75	108,128.00	3,906,665
iShares DJ Euro STOXX 50	Barclays GI	0.15%	quarterly	20	149,637	4,830.48	92,900.00	3,368,483
Dow Jones Euro STOXX 50 EX	IndExchange Investment AG	0.15%	annual	3	18,135	598.42	94,397.51	3,460,613
EasyETF Euro STOXX 50 A	AXA IM, BNP Paribas	0.45%	annual (cap.)	2	43,197	145.89	20,339.60	76,477
EasyETF Euro STOXX 50 B	AXA IM, BNP Paribas	0.25%	annual	2	19,623	683.51	1,117.80	40,801
UBS ETF DJ EURO STOXX 50 I	UBS ETF	0.10%	half-yearly					

Reported volumes traded in 2005 computed on daily averages. Whole figures for ETF DJ EURO STOXX 50 I was not available.

CHAPTER 2
Understanding how ETFs operate

Define ETFs

Exchange-Traded Funds (ETFs), are baskets of securities that are traded, just like individual stocks, via a brokerage firm on the stock exchange. ETFs Shares are traded by other investors that also go through brokerage firms to enable their transactions. Trading all-day makes the ETF assets more flexible compared to the open-end mutual funds who are their familiar sister, where the investors are limited to be patient until the end of the day before they can directly buy/sell shares with a mutual fund firm. Investors can buy or sell ETF assets throughout the trading day as long as the stock exchanges are open. Either way, you could trade a stock, you could also trade an ETF. Investors can sell shares short or buy them on margin. This makes these great investment mediums useful for institutional investors and those traders who are often looking to hedge equity positions quickly. A clear difference between ETF assets and the conventional open-end mutual funds is that the ETFs don't trade necessarily at the net asset value (NAV). Which are the combined cash holdings and the market value of the underlying security. Even though the supply and demand for ETF asset shares is facilitated by the values and performance of the underlying securities in the particular index that they track, other factors can and do influence the ETF asset market value. Like, the market value for ETF asset shares is considered by the forces of supply and demand for the ETF shares, and also the price gets off track occasionally from those of the underlying prices in the fund. But not by a big margin. The ETF assets have a mechanism that regulates the price discrepancy and stops premiums or discounts from becoming persistent or large. The discrepancy experienced between the ETF values and their underlying prices comes up with a potential profit opportunity for a particular set of people (investors). The market value of an ETF asset is maintained close to its NAV by enabling a few big institutional investors also known as the authorized participants (AP) to redeem or purchase ETF asset shares in-kind, this means using the underlying securities and not with cash. So when a small value discrepancy happens between an ETF asset and its underlying securities, the APs carry out a risk-free arbitrage trade. The arbitrage trade then enables the APs to exchange individual securities for huge blocks of ETF asset shares and the other way round. The arbitrage trade brings the market value of ETF asset shares to align with the fund's correct price and also helps to bring the Apasm maximum profit. The arbitrage trade can occur very fast and is very effective in maintaining ETF asset shares aligned with the correct value.

ETF assets are structured just like the open-end mutual funds. But, the companies which issue the ETF shares have agreed with the Securities and Exchange Commission (SEC) that they won't market or advertise their products as mutual funds in general or as open-end mutual funds. They are advertised only as exchange-traded securities and exchange-traded funds. According to the Security and Exchange Commission, mutual funds are granted and redeemed by mutual funds firms directly dealing with the public. The issuers of the ETF do not directly deal with the public. They only buy and sell from the APs. As a regulation, the advertising materials and prospectuses for ETF assets must state that individual ETF asset shareholders don't buy/sell shares directly with a fund firm and prominently disclose that fact. If individual shareholders receive shares on a stock exchange, they are buying a section of a creation unit that is owned by an Authorized Participant. If this sounds complicated, do not worry. After going through this book you will understand how ETF assets operations. Actually, you will more likely understand more about these distinctive investments in which a big number of advisers are in the business of financial services.

How ETFs work

The most common and straightforward ETF assets are those based on an indexing method, that simply aims to track the returns of a particular index. For instance, a rise or fall of 2% in the index should result in a rise or fall of roughly 2% for an ETF asset that tracks that particular index.

ETF assets are not directly traded with a fund management firm. But, are purchased or sold at any given time during the stock market trading time through a stockbroker directly. The ETFs' open-ended nature enables for the issuing and redemption of shares that are in the underlying fund to meet the investor needs.

ETFs' Potential benefits

The ETFs have some very distinctive features which may make them very useful for some investors, which may include liquidity, transparency and low costs (depending on broker's fees). In the same way to conventional index mutual funds, index ETF can also offer diversification in the kind of holding the wider market, as compared to focusing risk in just a few holdings

Liquidity
This is the ability to create and redeeming ETF securities regularly which ensures the underlying depth of liquidity. Different from the mutual funds, the ETF assets can be traded at market values through the entire trading day, at a value quoted on the SE.

Transparency
With transparent and straightforward index ETFs, the ETF asset issuer offers information daily to the market which includes a close representation of the ETF portfolio or the ETF basket, and the NAV of the ETF asset – making them a highly open and transparent investment alternative.

Costs
The yearly fees for the index ETFs are averagely less than many traditional index funds and significantly less than managed funds actively. But you will be required to put into consideration the whole 'all in' cost of putting cash in ETFs to know if they are the right for a given portfolio or client. This is because ETF assets also include the costs that are associated with the stock market trading, like the bid-offer spreads and broker commissions (or flat fees).

Diversification
A representative sample or Index funds invest in all of the securities in an index, offering a highly diversified investment. This provides investors access to a broad range of investments and scale of which an individual investor may not be able to access.

Tax efficiency
Buyers and sellers usually trade Exchange-Traded Funds units on the SE, without requiring to interact with the provider of the ETF. This shows that the transaction-oriented taxes, like stamp duty, are often lower. And in the same way, the tendency of ETFs to have a lower portfolio turnover compared to many funds that are managed actively. It means that there are usually fewer transactions and as a result of potentially low taxes that flows through to the ETF asset holders.

CHAPTER 3
Best ETF trading (making money) strategies

Dollar-Cost Averaging

This is the most basic strategy. It is a technique where on a regular schedule you buy a given fixed-dollar amount of an asset, without looking at the changing value of the given asset. The beginner investors are usually the young people that have been in the workforce for at least a year or two and have saved a little every month from their earnings. Those kinds of people can invest a few hundred dollars monthly in an ETF or a group of ETFs, instead of putting it in a savings account that is low-interest.

There are two major benefits to this kind of periodic investing.

1. The first one is that it inculcates a kind of discipline to your savings process. As most financial managers recommend, this makes sense to have yourself paid, and that is what you achieve when you save on a regular basis.
2. Secondly, it is that when you invest a similar fixed-dollar amount monthly in an ETF, you will compound more units if the ETF value is low and you accumulate fewer units when the price of the ETF is high, and as a result, it averages out the value of your holdings. With time, this method can handsomely pay off, you just have to remain disciplined.

For instance, say you invested $500 USD in the SPDR S&P 500 ETF (SPY) on the 1st of every month from 2016 September to 2019 August. SPY tracks the S&P 500 index. Thus, at the time the ETF units were priced at $136.16 USD in 2016 September, $500 USD would give you returns of 3.67 units, but 3 years later, when those units were priced close to $200 USD, an investment of $500 USD a month would have given you returns of 2.53 units. Through the 3-year period, you would have bought a total of 103.79 units of the SPY ETF (this is basing on closing prices that are adjusted for splits and dividends). At the closing value of $210.59 USD on 17 Aug 2019, those units would be worth $21,857.14 USD, for an annual average return of about 13%.

Asset Allocation

It means the allocation of a part of a portfolio to various asset categories such as bonds, stocks, cash, and commodities to ensure diversification, which is a very powerful investing vehicle. For most ETFs a lower investment threshold—

generally as low as $50 USD a month—makes it simple for anyone to execute a basic asset allocation method, depending on his/her investment risk tolerance and time horizon. For instance, an investor maybe 100 percent invested in the equity ETFs at the beginning just because of their high-risk tolerance and long investment time horizons. But as they gain more experience in the investment field and embark on key lifecycle, they are likely to shift to an investment mix that is less aggressive with 60 percent in equities ETFs and 40 percent in the bond ETFs.

Use ETFs to Gain Exposure to an Industry

Assuming you are not interested in investing in a market as much as a specific sector. Is producing clean coal the next "green"? It could be that a coal mining ETF asset is the next big thing. It could be a defense, technology or even financials, it is just very easy to purchase a sector ETF asset as compared to trying to corner the market in the industry equities.

Foreign ETF Assets Enable You to Access the International Markets

Making foreign investments can be very complicated. Foreign tax laws, currency adjustments, and the whole overseas issues. However, some of the ETFs make the foreign investment much easier to make. Domestic currency-based International market ETF assets, the advent market ETFs, the broad foreign funds, and ETFs that track individual nations such as China and Brazil as well. There is no reason to fear to make your investment outside the United States or any country any longer.

Invest in Commodities

The truth is that you don't have enough room in your home to store for barrels of oil, chests of gold, or cattle. Or maybe you do but you do plenty of room in your portfolio to accommodate all these commodities ETFs. So invest in commodities without investing in commodities or simply without stocking up cattle, you could buy a commodity ETF and have exposure instantly to the market. It is much easier to transaction this way, and you don't need to feed it

Bond ETFs are a Gift that Just Keeps on Giving

These ETFs are a bit more enticing compared to most other investments since aside from trading on the secondary markets, they are also capable to add a revenue stream to your portfolio.

Generally, bond investing can be a little difficult. Default risk, coupon rates, duration. Nevertheless, a bond ETF could address some of those difficulties by offering investors a single pre-packaged asset which provides instant access to the bond market

Exchange-Traded Notes

ETFs have variations known as the ETNs (exchange-traded notes). Exchange-Traded Notes are assets that are issued as senior debt notes by a major bank – a contrast to the ETFs that are composed of securities like currencies, commodities, forwards, options and futures.

When you purchase an Exchange-Traded Note, you purchase a debt asset that is the same as a bond, although the agreement of the debt contract is decided by the note's structure. ETNs are supported by a major bank that has a higher credit rating, and so you get more secure products. However, the ETNs also have their own credit risk, it is just that it is at a lower level.

Trade the Currency Market with ETFs

ETNs and Bond ETFs are 2 ways that you can invest in the interest rate market, although when it comes to the international interest rate trading, you have to look no further than the currency ETF assets. Whether you are looking to invest in a regional currency such as Europe, a broad currency asset, or even an individual country's currency, then you can count on ETFs literally. The currency ETFs are an ideal strategy to play foreign interest rates, hedge foreign risk, or invest in international currencies.

Trade ETFs on the Downside

Every trade you buy, there is trade selling on the other side. Most investors identify investing with just buying, but that is only 50% of every position. So you should understand that there are other ETFs that are specifically there for the bearish investors.

Selling any ETF is creating the downside, but you should understand that you can purchase an ETF and still be short. That is referred to as an inverse ETF asset. It is perfect for those investors who are restricted against selling, but still want to go short; you can just buy an inverse ETF asset

Hedging Risk with ETFs

Again, we come back to "investing means buying." But a big part of investing is also protecting against risk. That's where ETFs can help. Do you have a large diversified portfolio that wins when the market rises? Protect the downside by selling a market ETF. Short a lot of oil stocks? Buy an oil ETF to protect your upside exposure. Long an index? Protect your position by selling an underlying ETF.

Hedging

It is demonstrated in the above point, but the ETFs are an ideal way to cover the index positions. Say you are long a certain index; you could make an opposite trade to cover your risk. Other indexes are tracked with numerous ETFs, so opportunities can be many if you are looking to hedge the index risk. You could trade ETFs to cover some or all your index trades or in other cases just put on the same index position by the use of an ETF. At the end of the day, that is why they are there.

Consider ETF Options

ETF options can be utilized in so many ways. They can be used to hedge ETFs and the other way or correlating index. The ETF calls could be ideal assets to get upside exposure without risking too much of your money, and puts are a way that you can get short also. You can apply advanced ETF asset option strategies to take a position that is volatility or maybe trade for market price. If you have an ETF asset that lists the options, there you go, then you have options.

Trade Earnings Season with ETFs

Four times at least per year, you are going to prepare for the earnings season. ETF assets could help you with that strategy. Even if you use ETFs to go long a promising industry, cover against the earnings surprises, or just trading earnings volatility with ETF asset option, then there is an earning strategy just for you. If you have

Trade ETFs Which Fit Your Investment Style

Do you tend to like investing in value stocks? Do you like the large-cap securities? But either way, there is always an ETF reserved for you. Be it value blend, or growth, or even small, mid, large-cap there is an ETF that fits your strategy. It is imperative that you be comfortable with your portfolio, and style the ETFs to fit your investment style.

Swing Trading

These are trades that aim to benefit from sizeable swings in the stocks or any other instruments such as commodities or currencies. This kind of trades could run from anywhere in a few days to weeks to get to the intended prices, as opposed to day trades that are rarely left open for more than a day.

Features of ETF assets that make them ideal for swing trading are the diversification and the tight bid or ask spreads. Also, because ETFs are accessible for a broad range of industries and most different investment classes, if you are just beginning out, you can decide to trade an ETF asset that is sector-based or based on an asset class that they have some knowledge or expertise. For instance, if you have a technological background you may benefit trading in a technology ETF such as the Invesco QQQ (QQQ) ETF, that replicate the Nasdaq-100 index. If you are just starting out and you closely follow the commodity markets you may want to get into one of the different commodity ETFs that are available, like the (DBC) ETF that tracks the Invesco DB Commodity. Since ETFs are more of baskets of several stocks or different other assets, they may not necessarily replicate a similar degree of upward value movement as just one stock in a bull market would. Diversification makes them not very susceptible than just a single stock to a huge downward move.

Sector Rotation

The ETFs make it quite easy for anyone starting out in executing industry rotation, based on different levels of the economic cycle.

For instance, say you have been investing in the biotech industry via the iShares Nasdaq Biotech (IBB) ETF. With this ETF up by 137% in a period of five years this is as of 2018 Jan 31st, you may wish to lock in the profits in the ETF and rotate to a rather defensive industry such as consumer staples through the Consumer Staples Select industry SPDR ETF (XLP).

Selling Short

This is the selling of a borrowed financial instrument or security; it is normally quite risky for most people and thus not something that if you are starting off should do. However, because of the lower risk of a short squeeze, it is more preferred compared to shorting individual stocks and the significantly low cost of borrowing as well (instead of the cost that is incurred when you try to short a stock that has a high short interest). The risk-mitigation is very important for everyone considering to start short selling.

ETFs have many attributes that make them great instruments if you are starting out as a trader and investor. Some Exchange-Traded Funds trading strategies mostly suitable if you are starting out are the dollar-cost averaging, swing trading, asset allocation, short selling, sector rotation, hedging, and seasonal trends.

CHAPTER 4
ETF structure and asset class issues

DEFINING THE MARKET

Among the most fundamental falsehoods in the ETF market is the term "ETF". The truth is, when most individuals say "ETF," they are really talking about "ETP," (exchange-traded product).

Most products trading under "ETF" does not fund, instead, they are notes, trusts, commodity pools, or some other structures. Even the very first ETF in the U.S. (SPY) is a grantor trust and not a fund at all.

As much as this may sound as minutiae, you should understand the different structures in the Exchange-Traded Product space, it could help you to avoid unwelcome surprises and unnecessary risks.

Exchange-Traded Product (ETP)

An ETP is a pooled securities medium which trades on a SE and has continuous creation or redemption mechanism, that allows the number of outstanding shares to vary based on the investor demand. Exchange-Traded Products conform to different legal structures.

If ETP is used in this manner, then it explicitly excludes the closed-end funds (CEF), that don't have a continuous creation or redemption way. Closed-End Funds are a very important and controversial investment medium but are excluded completely from this conversation.

Unit Investment Trust

It is an alternative product structure that is allowed under and regulated by the 1940 Act. Unit Investment Trusts share many attributes with the ETFs, although comes with some restrictions. Unit Investment Trusts ought to have a date for termination when the product will be either redeemed/canceled, but that date can be decades later in the future.

The important thing is, UIT is more passive compared to ETFs. According to the SEC, a UIT doesn't have corporate officers, an investment adviser or board of directors to render advice during the trust's life.

Practically, there are two major differences between ETFs and UITs:

1. UITs can replicate fully, buying all securities in the index that they track, instead of optimization, where a fund can purchase some but not all securities in a given index it tries to track them with the hopefull replication of the index's return.
2. UITs can't re-invest dividends that they receive but should hold them in cash between the quarterly distributions.
3. UITs can't participate in the lending of securities.

Some of the oldest and largest ETPs around the globe are UITs, including the PowerShares Nasdaq-100 QQQs and SPY.

Commodities Pool

Most currency and commodity funds that hold the futures contracts are regulated by commodities pools under the Commodity Futures Trading Commission (CFTC). They are regulated under the 1933 Act and not under the 1940 Act at all. Commodities pools are different from funds in several ways: You are not required to have independent boards or yearly meetings, for example. However, the biggest difference is how those structures are taxed.

Exchange-Traded Note

This is no way a fund, but it is a debt instrument that is given by an investment bank where the bank gives a promise to deliver a given pattern of profits to the note holder. An ETN may trade just like the ETF and may also be redeemed/created continuously, the note holder cannot claim the underlying assets that it is tracking. If the issuer of an Exchange-Traded Note goes bankrupt, the noteholders will be forced to be creditors in the firm. In short, ETNs are unsubordinated, unsecured debt.

Counterparty Risk

There discussion everywhere of counterparty risk in the ETP sector, but this is too often unclear and confused. For the shareholders of these products, there are 4 key sources of counterparty risk in the United States ETP structures.

Exchange-Traded Notes

ETN investors are vulnerable to the greatest potential counterparty risk. Trading in ETNs is very unsubordinated, unsecured debt notes. The whole price of the notes is based on the credit of the bank that is underwriting. If the underwriting bank goes under, then the investors join other bondholders in the line of creditors.

The Lehman Brothers, for example, had two Exchange-Traded Notes outstanding at the time when it filed for bankruptcy. Even though the products had very little assets, anyone that is left holding the notes on that day that the firm went bankrupt then they lost nearly all of their investment.

This kind of risk in Exchange-Traded Notes is limited because the notes can be redeemed back to the issuer, usually on a day-to-day basis. It may be stretched during the times the market is disrupted, but you still have a relatively faster pathway to redeem the securities at Net Asset Value on the basis of the creation unit.

Swaps

Other ETFs, and to be specific the inverse/leveraged ETFs and some commodity pools, use swaps to access the market. A swap is a contract that is privately negotiated whereby two parties accept to exchange a given pattern of profits; this is, at a fee, the bank will accept to give a fund with twice the daily move as the S&P 500.

Most investors overstate the stage of counterparty risk in a swap contract, let's say the fund hands-over the full value of its investment to the counterparty. What will happen is the two counterparties in a swap don't exchange any cash first; they will have to wait until the market can move by a given amount that the now swap counterparty will post the cash. With this said, the amount at risk in a swap contract is limited to the amount of movement between the posting of collateral of the underlying securities.

Other swaps need to be settled daily; others will extend even further out. An investor who is concerned should get to the root of the specific policy of the issuer of the given ETF.

Derivatives

Most ETPs apply derivative instruments to get market exposure. The derivatives may include either those listed (options, futures, etc.) or over-the-counter (OTC) derivatives. Those that are listed have limited counterparty risk because any agreements are assured by the clearinghouse that hosts the trade or exchange. Over-the-counter derivatives don't share any pre-written assurances, and therefore are pronto the complete value in counterparty risk.

Securities Lending

Securities lending activity is the final key source of counterparty risk. Most true ETFs participate in securities lending as a way to improve their returns.

In this kind of activity, a fund lends out securities that it holds to the investors interested in selling them short. For example, the iShares S&P 500 (IVV) ETF understands the ownership of a large quantity of Exxon-Mobil (XOM) stock, and will continue to do so for the foreseeable future. If an individual wants to short this stock XOM, IVV (ETF) may lend out those shares to that particular short-seller. In return, IVV will charge a fee, and collateral as well usually equal to 102% of what the loan is worth. The ETF may invest the collateral in other kinds of securities. The individual short selling will need to post some more collateral if at all the position goes against them, to keep up with the 102% hedge.

An efficiently run securities lending program could earn good returns for its investors. It doesn't go, however, without any risk.

The main risk is not anything that you would predict: the borrower will go missing and not give up the shares. Even with this happening, the risk is countered by the requirements of the collateral. The challenge comes if the collateral is invested aggressively by the fund firm itself; if that gives investment goes bad, the fund is also likely to lose money. Even if there are regulations on what kinds of securities are embraced as collateral, the regulations are not as airtight. And still, this risk is de minimis: Index Universe thinks it is something that no ETF end-investor has ever to lose money because of a securities lending issue. Some firms encountered challenges during the bankruptcy of Lehman, but those losses were low and every company made its shareholder complete.

TAX RISK

ETFs are commonly known for being tax-efficient mediums for investments and are: Compared to conventional mutual funds, for example, ETFs will rarely pay out its capital gains of any size of the distributions.

Even though, the investors can encounter afoul of serious tax consequences especially if they don't know the difference of how ETFs are taxed on the basis of the asset. This is most true when you break from fixed-income and conventional equity buckets. Most investors are not familiar with the tax treatment of currencies, derivative-based instruments, and commodities.

ETF TAX PRIMER

An ETP's tax treatment is concerned with both its particular structure and the asset class that it covers. An asset class of a given fund can be categorized in one of five classifications: fixed income, equities, currencies, alternatives, and commodities. For the purposes of taxes, ETPs come in one of the 5 structures: unit investment trusts, open-ended funds, limited partnerships (LPs), exchange-traded notes and grantor trusts.

It should be noted that these structures are not aligned with the legal structures that are mentioned above, as two (LPs and grantor trust) which are tax only structures. Many of the LPs are commodity ETFs that hold futures, many of the grantor trusts are physical commodity ETFs.

Fixed-Income and Equity ETFs

Fixed-income and equity ETFs are very familiar. It does not matter the structure they hold, the gains obtained when a sale is made are taxed at for short-term holdings ordinary income rates of less than 12 months and as a long-term capital gain for long-term holding periods, this is more than 12 months. It makes the max tax rate for the long-term gains of 1%, under the current law.

Commodity ETFs

This is even more complicated, as commodity Exchange-Traded Funds may be structured in three different ways: LPs, ETNs, or grantor trusts.

Grantor trust structures are meant for the physically held precious metals ETFs, like the iShares Silver Trust (SLV) and the SPDR Gold Trust (GLD). These and other related funds store the real commodity in vaults while giving investors exposure to spot the returns. Under IRS rules currently, investing in the precious metals ETFs is considered to be collectibles. Meaning they don't qualify for the 15% tax rate that is applied to the conventional equity investments; rather, long-term profits are taxed at a max rate of 28 percent. If the shares are held for less than a year, profits are taxed like ordinary income maximum of 35%.

Most of the ETFs hold futures agreement to get exposure to commodities and are structured like the LPs. Commodity funds that are structured as LPs include the United States Natural Gas Fund (UNG) and PowerShares DB Commodity Fund (DBC). Funds that are based on Futures have distinctive tax consequences. 60 percent of any profits are taxed at the long-haul capital profits rate of 15%, and the other 40% is taxed at the ordinary income rate for the investors, notwithstanding how long they hold the shares. This results in a blended max cap gain rate at 23%.

ETFs in a limited partnership is seen as pass-through kind of investments, so any profits that the trust makes are at the end of the year marked-to-market and are passed on to the investors, thus creating a taxable event. This means that your cost basis adjusts at year-end and you can be subject to pay taxes on gains regardless of whether you sold your shares or not.

For tax reporting, limited partnership ETFs also generate a Schedule K-1 form. This can create uncertainty and annoyance for the average investor not familiar with K-1s when they receive these forms in the mail.

Commodity ETNs do not hold the physical commodity, nor do they hold futures contracts; they are, as mentioned earlier, simply debt notes. As a result, commodity ETNs are currently taxed like equity and/or bond funds. Long-term gains are taxed at 15%, while short-term gains are taxed as ordinary income (max 35%). Despite the fact that many of these products track futures-based indexes, they do not generate a K-1.

Currency ETFs

Currency ETPs come in one of four structures: open-end funds, grantor trusts, limited partnerships or ETNs.

WisdomTree is currently the only issuer to offer currency ETFs structured as open-end funds. The WisdomTree Dreyfus Japanese Yen Fund (JYF) and WisdomTree Dreyfus Euro Fund (EU) are some of their funds. These funds have short-term instruments of the money-market debt denominated in the local currencies; different products can handle repos that are collateralized. The tax implications for the funds are the same as the equity funds. The WisdomTree's prospectuses believe that profits if held for more than a year, are taxed as long-term capital gains of 15%; that is if it is held for a year or less, profits are taxed maximum 35% as ordinary income.

The Currency Shares of Rydex are organized as grantor trusts. Every Currency Shares product offers investors exposure to the underlying currency's spot exchange rates by holding foreign currency in their bank accounts. Taxation of Currency Shares is quite easy and straight-forward. All the profits that come from the selling of shares are ordinary income taxed at a maximum of 35%, no matter the period of time that the investor holds them.

Same as the commodity LP funds, this currency funds which hold the futures agreements are structured as LPs. The funds may include the Bullish Funds and the PowerShares DB US Dollar Index Bearish (UUP and UDN, respectively) and also leveraged currency funds like ProShares UltraShort Yen Fund (YCS) and the Pro-Shares Ultra-Short Euro Fund (EUO). Tax effects of the currency limited partnership Exchange-Traded Funds are similar to those of the commodity limited partnership Exchange-Traded Funds—profits subject to a similar 60/40 blend, no matter the period the shares are held. These are also marked-to-market and are reported on K-1s at year-end.

Uncertainties that come with the taxation of currency ETNs. Because of an IRS ruling that was passed towards the end of 2007. gains from the currency ETNs can now be taxed at a maximum of 35% as ordinary income generally, no matter the period of time that the investor holds the shares. However, as per the prospectuses of other currency ETNs, investors can classify gains to be long-term cap gains if a genuine election is made before the end of the day that the ETN was purchased under Section 988.

Types of Exchange-Traded Portfolios

ETF VS mutual funds is a debate that is ongoing and is likely to never end. There are detractors and supporters on both sides, and if these products will still be present, investors will continue to invest trillions in both of them. Each one of them has its benefits and downsides, but that is another day's discussion.

Now, let us check out some common types of ETFs.

Equity Funds

Many Exchange-Traded Funds track industry or equity indexes. Other index ETFs track an index as a whole, while others go through representative sampling, that slightly deviates by the use of the option, swap contracts, and futures and buying of stocks in other instances that may not be found in the index. In case this sampling becomes too aggressive, it could lead you to track errors. An ETF that has a tracking error with more than 2% can be considered to be actively managed.

As the ETFs get more and more advanced, it is something that investors should look out for.

The proliferation of Exchange-Traded Funds offers the investors with an affordable way to diversify their portfolios. Whether you are looking to capture a specific sector of the global stocks, a wider sector or just a niche market, then there is an Exchange-Traded Fund asset just for that. In addition, some invest in different sized companies, you could be after the small-cap, mid-cap or large-cap fund. Aside from there being funds for almost any sector that you want to make your investment, and having more that is coming to the market weekly, there are also those that use various styles like growth or value or investing.

With plenty of alternatives out there, it is imperative that you determine first the equity of your portfolio's allocation and then, you can select ETF assets based on those decisions, which meet your investment goals.

Fixed-Income Funds

Many financial professionals advise that you invest just a part of your portfolio in fixed-income securities like bond ETFs and bonds. Since bonds seem to bring down the volatility of a portfolio while offering an additional stream of income as well. The age-old question becomes part of the percentages. How much should you invest in equities, cash or fixed income? This is popularly known as asset allocation. For equity funds, many bond funds are available. If you are an Investor you are not sure of what kind to invest in then you should think about the total bond-market ETFs that invest in the whole United States bond market.

Commodity Funds

Before you can invest in the commodity ETF assets, it is imperative that you understand why you are interested in the commodities first. Historically, the commodities market had very little value correlation with equities. Professionals say strategic asset allocation constitutes 90 % of the return of a portfolio. However, it is not sufficient to have bonds, stocks, commodities, real estate and cash in your portfolio. You have to diversify within each of those asset classes as well. That is where the Exchange-Traded Funds come in. Investors can purchase a commodity ETF that tracks the value changes of certain commodities such as oil or gold, or in a commodity stock ETF which invests in common shares of producers of a commodity. The former has very little correlation to the stocks, while the latter is highly correlated to the stocks. In case your portfolio already has equities, then a straight commodity ETF makes more sense.

Currency Funds

With the increase in volatility of the world's currencies to the USD's role as a reserve currency is slowly by slowly fading away, investors that want to cover the value of a USD denominated investment they have to get options that will hedge against the depreciating dollar. An option is to invest equally in foreign stock ETFs or foreign stocks. However, it will not offer you an asset class diversification since foreign stocks correlate highly with the U.S. stocks. A better option would be to put your investment in foreign currency ETFs. Whether you are looking at a single currency or a broader focus one, the aim is to cover your portfolio from the depreciating USD. And, if the USD is appreciating and you have invested in foreign stocks, you could cover the value of these holdings by going short on the same currency ETF asset.

It is imperative for you to remember that if you invest in the currency then it should represent a small part of the overall investment, this is to soften the risk of currency volatility.

Real Estate Funds

If you are an income investor and still want a little sizzle with your steak you might consider investing in real estate investment trust ETFs (REIT). You might choose a fund which invests in a given kind of real estate or an investment that is wider in nature, the best attraction of this kind of fund is because they should pay out about 90% of the taxable income to the shareholders. It makes them so attractive in terms of the returns, despite the increase in volatility when you compare with the bonds. These kinds of funds are a very excellent source of income, mostly for the short-term interest rates and inflation are near historic lows.

Specialty Funds

As the ETFs became more and more popular, a number of funds come to meet all conceivable investment strategy, more like what happened to mutual funds. Two of the most interesting ones are the inverse funds, which gain when a given index does not perform well, and leveraged funds, that can double or triple your returns of a given index by applying leverage. You could even purchase ETF assets that can do both. If you decide to dabble in inverse ETFs or leveraged, it is imperative that you comprehend the risks involved. All in all, they are so unreliable and volatile as long-term investments.

Quick Note on ETFs vs. Mutual Funds

Originally, ETFs were created to offer investors with a more liquid product and tax-efficient compared to mutual funds. While ETF assets are passive in nature, because they have become more widely accepted, financial managers have come up with funds that are actively managed, albeit the higher management charges, that seek to outdo the indexes. When choosing an investment, whether it is an ETF or a mutual fund, the main concern should be the amount you pay to so as to own it. Considering that many investment managers underperform their benchmarks, it is important that you thoroughly consider the benefits and the downside of these funds before you can make an investment.

Every mutual fund and ETF can track errors. The profits of the two products when you track the same index are within few basis points generally. For many individuals, it is really what makes sense in the given situation. If you are a do-it-yourself investor, then ETF assets would probably make much sense. If you make a monthly contribution to an automatic investment plan, then mutual funds are likely to be your preference. But it is important that you understand why and what you are purchasing.

Ever since the S&P 500 was introduced Depository Receipts in 1993, popularly known as spiders (SPDR), ETFs have exploded. Currently, the mass appeal looks like it is unstoppable. While they are not for everyone, they can certainly help to diversify your portfolio.

CHAPTER 5
Conclusion and Perspectives

Exchange-Traded Funds are open-end index funds which trade just like the regular stocks on the SEs. They are a combination of closed-end funds and the features of conventional mutual funds since new shares are continuously created/redeemed and the outstanding shares trade all day on the SEs. The ETFs were launched initially in the North-American markets in the early 1990s and new listings on the exchanges resulted in 450+ various ETFs that were traded across the globe with a steady increase in assets that were under management. Interestingly, the growth in the volume traded of these instruments has generated. Major ETFs in the U.S., are traded more than other security. The European ETF markets are young, although they demonstrate the same tendencies, and have fierce competition between the exchanges for order flow and issuers for the new cash. The success of the ETF raises the issue of the structure of mutual fund trading. The research on the ETFs mostly addresses on their performance and efficiency as well as on their influence on the other markets. As compared to the closed-end funds, the particular in-kind creation/redemption process makes sure a higher level of value efficiency. Nonetheless, the benefits inherent to the process (in-kind) do not assist the ETF managers to offer higher performance on a no-load least-cost index mutual funds. All in all, the emergent of ETFs improves the liquidity of the single stock creating the efficiency of index derivatives markets and the benchmark indices. Lastly, ETF assets have a significant role, even though not quite a prominent role in the value discovery process. Aside from the rising importance of the ETFs markets, the literature on this subject is still rare to come by. However, research perspectives are very promising. For instance, Asian and European ETFs markets are extremely active but are still a research area that is almost untouched. The empirical, as well as the theory of the competition between ETFs tracking the same index and between marketplaces. Regulation problems should be included in future research as the ETF markets' evolution may lead regulators and markets to adapt to the new rules. Finally, the new kinds of ETF assets are launched regularly and a study has yet to show their trading, specificities or uses for the ETF derivatives and fixed-income ETFs.

www.ingramcontent.com/pod-product-compliance
Lightning Source LLC
Chambersburg PA
CBHW030558220526
45463CB00007B/3113